THE BEST AFTER DINNER JOKES

GORDON TRUEMAN

with illustrations by
DAVID MYERS

With my very best wishes to you for your health and happiness Always. Gordon Trueman.

ONE-O-ONE BOOKS

© Gordon Trueman 1997
All Rights Reserved. No part of this publication may be reproduced, stored in a retrieval system, nor transmitted in any form or by any means, whether electronic, mechanical, photocopying, recording, or otherwise, without prior written permission from the publisher.

First published in 1997 by One-O-One Books,
177 Vauxhall Bridge Road, London, SW1V 1EU

British Library Cataloguing in Publication Data
A CIP record for this book is available from the British Library

ISBN 0 9531692 0 0

Printed and bound in the United Kingdom by
MFP Design & Print, Manchester

CONTENTS

HAPPY FAMILIES 5
ANIMAL CRACKERS 9
MEDICAL MEN 16
NEXT APPLICANT PLEASE! 18
BRUSHES WITH THE LAW 20
A MATTER OF TASTE 22
DEMON DRINK 25
NIGHT CLUBBING 27
THE OPEN ROAD 29
ALL AT SEA 33
ON A WING AND A PRAYER 35
HOME FROM HOME 37
FANCY THAT! 41
PARTING SHOTS 45
101 SAYINGS 49

Dear Reader

EVER SINCE MY early childhood I have always enjoyed a good laugh. As I grew up I realised the joy, pleasure and laughter which a good joke can bring. They do say that three laughs a day help to reduce heart attacks and relieve tension and if this is so then I hope this book will help you to achieve this.

Before I begin, I'd like to tell you a little bit about myself.

1929 was a really good year for me. It was the year I was born – on May 23rd to be exact. Years ago it was an easy date to remember, because it was the day before Empire Day when we all had a day off.

I was born in Birkenhead in Cheshire to very loving and caring parents. My two brothers, Cecil and Charles, were ten and six years older than me. Though we were poor, we were a very happy family, sharing a large house with many other families, all having our own rooms and – believe it or not – one toilet, which was outside in the back garden.

When I was four, we moved to a terraced house. This was absolute luxury, even though it still had an outside toilet and the bath was a galvanised tub under the stairs. During the War we used it as our bomb shelter. Like many other children I was evacuated. Although I missed my parents I was very well looked after by my foster parents, the Bennett family, on their farm near Llanidloes, Montgomeryshire in Wales, where I learnt how to milk cows, ride horses and 'round up' cattle.

At 16, I served an apprenticeship as a motor mechanic, before joining the Royal Navy as a stoker mechanic, serving on seven ships in all and establishing many friendships.

Whilst on home leave, I met my lovely wife, Betty, who has been and is still a great loving inspiration in every way. I could not wish for a better partner and am very proud of our only son, Colin, who has presented us with a lovely daughter-in-law, Pat, and two adored grandchildren, Thomas and Sophie.

Finally, I would like to thank everyone who has helped or contributed in any way to the production of this book, especially David Myers for his splendid illustrations.

Happiness to you all.

Gordon Trueman.

HAPPY FAMILIES

A WIFE WAS so annoyed with her husband coming home late every night from his club, usually having had one too many, she decided to teach him a lesson. So she dressed herself up as the Devil and hid in an alleyway waiting for her husband to come past on his way home. All of a sudden, she heard him singing as he approached in the dark. As he passed by, she jumped out in front of him and shouted: 'Boo, I'm the Devil!' He was not at all startled but simply held out his hand and said: 'How do you do. I'm married to your sister!'

☺ ● ☺ ● ☺

AN ESKIMO BOY was out fishing in a hole in the ice near to his igloo when he heard a call from his mother: 'Hurry up dear, your dinner's on the table and you're missing Vera Lynn on the television.' 'Oh no,' the boy shouted back, 'not whale meat again!'

A LITTLE BOY was staying with his grandad for the holidays and one day asked him: 'Were you in the War, Grandad?' 'Yes,' his grandfather replied. 'Have you any trophies from the War?' the little boy asked. 'Well, I used to have a rifle but I had to hand it back.' 'What about a tin helmet?' 'I did have, but I had to hand that back as well.' 'A gas mask?' 'I had to give that back also.' 'So haven't you anything from your days in the War?' 'Oh yes, I've still got my big army great-coat.' 'Oh,' said the boy, 'Can I see it?' 'Certainly. It's upstairs in the loft next to the tank.' The little boy jumped up excitedly, 'You mean you've got a tank as well!'

☺ • ☺ • ☺

A YOUNG BOY was walking home from school one day when he came across a guy struggling to carry an old sofa out of his house. 'Do you need a hand with that?' asked the boy. 'No, I'm only getting rid of it,' the guy replied, 'You can have it if you want.' The boy thought that the sofa would look good in his own bedroom, so off he trundled, the proud owner of a new piece of furniture. When he got home, though, his father angrily demanded: 'What are you doing with that sofa?' 'I thought it would be nice for my room,' the boy replied. 'Who gave it to you?' 'This man said I could have it.' 'What have I always told you,' shouted his father, clipping his son across the ear, 'never accept suites from strangers.'

☺ • ☺ • ☺

A GUY WAS thinking of getting married, so he asked his best friend, who had been married many years for some advice. 'What would be your definition of marriage?' he asked. His friend thought very deeply for a few moments and then said: 'Marriage is a three-ringed circus. One is an engagement ring, two is a wedding ring and three is her pestering!'

HAPPY FAMILIES

A MAN AND his wife had been very happily married for many years until suddenly, out of the blue, they had an argument and decided that rather than talk to each other, they would leave each other notes. This worked very well until one day the husband left a note for his wife on his way up to bed saying: *I have an urgent appointment in the morning at 8 am. Will you please give me a call at 6 am.* Next morning, still half asleep, he saw from his clock that it was 10 am. Leaping out of bed, he shouted across to his wife: 'I asked you to call me at 6 am!' 'Haven't you read the note I left you?' she replied. He looked at the note which read: *It's 6 am. Time for you to get up.*

☺ ● ☺ ● ☺

A GUY HAD been married for twenty-five years and, on the day of his Wedding Anniversary, he said to his wife: 'I'd like to cook a meal for you tonight, what would you like?' 'Well,' she replied, 'Do you remember our honeymoon in Paris, when we had that lovely meal of escargots?' 'OK,' he told her, 'you relax while I go out and buy some and come back to cook them.' Off he went to the shops where he bought a very large bag of snails. On his way home, he bumped into an old friend he hadn't seen for years. 'Come and have a drink, for old time's sake,' the friend said. Three hours later the guy looked at his watch. 'Gosh! Is that the time?' he said, 'I must go, my wife is waiting for her meal.' He rushed off home, but when he got there, he'd had so much to drink that he couldn't find his key. As he was fumbling at the door, the bag with all the snails in fell out of his hand and broke open on the doorstep. Hearing all this, his wife came to the door. 'Where have you been?' she asked angrily, 'How could you be late home tonight!' 'But, dear,' he replied, trying to coax the snails through the door, 'You'll never believe the hard time I've had shepherding this lot home!'

☺ ● ☺ ● ☺

TWO GUYS HAVING a nice quiet drink were talking about their families. 'Do any of your family have nicknames?' one of them asked. 'Yes. My wife. She's known as Encyclopaedia.' 'Encyclopaedia? Why's that?' 'Because she knows everything!'

A MAN TURNED up at his local veterinary surgery with his two dogs. 'What's the problem?' asked the vet. 'I'd like you to remove both of their tails.' 'That's quite in order, Sir, but, if you don't mind me asking, why do you want me to remove your two dogs' tails?' 'Well, you see, my mother-in-law is coming to stay and I don't want anyone showing her how pleased they are to see her.'

☺ ● ☺ ● ☺

AFTER 25 YEARS in the Navy a sailor came home to civilian life. 'Before we start our new life together,' he told his wife, 'I've got to be straight and honest with you. I was occasionally unfaithful when I was away from you in the Navy.' 'Oh, well,' she replied, 'I must say that I was also unfaithful, once or twice, while you were away.' They decided to let bygones be bygones and set about the daily chores. While his wife went out shopping the sailor did the housework. He was tidying under the stairs when he came across three eggs and £3,000 in cash. When his wife came home, he confronted her about the eggs and the money. 'Oh that's how I got paid – in eggs – for my infidelity,' she explained. 'Why three eggs?' asked her husband. 'Well, I only sold them when I had a dozen!'

☺ ● ☺ ● ☺

MICKEY MOUSE WALKED into this bed shop and told the assistant: 'I want to bring my water-bed back and change it for a mattress.' 'But you only purchased it last week,' the assistant replied, 'why do you want to change it?' 'Because ever since we bought it, Minnie and I have been drifting apart.'

☺ ● ☺ ● ☺

ANIMAL CRACKERS

A BULL MASTIFF and a collie were out walking on leads with their owners. While their owners were talking to each other, the bull mastiff said to the collie, 'Why don't you come out at night, it's great fun with lots of other dogs, we all meet in the park and have a wonderful time.' The collie replied: 'There's no way my owner would let me out at night on my own. How do you manage to get out?' 'It's easy,' said the bull mastiff, 'I just make a mess on the carpet and then my owner boots me out of the door.' 'Thanks,' said the collie, 'I'll try that tonight.' That night, the collie met the bull mastiff in the park and they both had a wonderful time. This carried on for about three months until one day when the collie suddenly stopped going out at night. Shortly afterwards, the bull mastiff met the collie again while they were out with their owners. 'Where have you been lately?' asked the bull mastiff. 'I'm not coming any more,' replied the collie. 'Why's that?' 'Well, to be honest, I'm fed up with getting a good hiding every night and I don't want to end up with a face like yours!'

A RABBIT WALKED into a greengrocer's shop and started rapping his claws on the counter. The owner of the shop came forward and said to the rabbit, who was still rapping his claws on the counter: 'Can I help you?' 'Yes,' said the rabbit, still rapping on the counter, 'Have you any carrots?' 'Yes,' replied the owner. 'I'll have a bag full, please.' The following day, the rabbit returned and, rapping his claws on the counter again, asked for another bag of carrots. The third day, back came the rabbit, rapping his claws on the counter, and ordering a bag of carrots. This time the owner had had enough. As he handed over a big bag of carrots he said: 'If you rap your claws on my counter again, I'll nail your paws to the counter.' The rabbit disappeared with the carrots. The next day, the rabbit returned. 'Have you any nails?' he asked. 'No,' said the owner. 'Right,' said the rabbit, immediately rapping his claws on the counter again, 'I'll have a bag of carrots.'

☺ • ☺ • ☺

A FIELD MOUSE walked into this Music Store. 'Can I help you?' enquired the assistant. 'Yes,' said the mouse, 'I'm looking for a mouse organ.' 'A mouse organ!' said the assistant, 'Funny you should say that, we had a mouse in here last week asking for exactly the same thing.' 'Oh,' replied the mouse, 'That must have been my sister, Harmonica.'

☺ • ☺ • ☺

A DEVOTED DOG owner became very upset one day when his dog's back legs gave in. Off he dashed to the veterinary surgery to see if anything could be done. After a long examination, the vet asked: 'How old is your dog?' 'Fourteen,' replied the owner. 'In that case I'm afraid there's nothing I can do. He's too old, I'll have to put him to sleep.' 'You can't do that!' pleaded the dog's owner, 'I love that dog. I've looked after him with loving care for 14 years. Surely there must be something you can do?' After a long pause, the vet said: 'Well, I could fit your dog with tin legs.' 'Tin legs!' replied the owner, 'I've never heard of anything like that before.' 'Well, you soon will,' the vet replied, 'when it goes running down your drive!'

ANIMAL CRACKERS

ONCE UPON A time, a mother skunk gave birth to two lovely baby skunks, who she decided to name 'In' and 'Out'. When they grew up, the mother skunk told them: 'In and Out, you can go out and play now.' So out they went. Shortly afterwards, the mother skunk looked out, only to see In misbehaving. 'In you come in and Out you stay out,' she called out. So In came in and Out stayed out. After quite a long penance had been served, the mother skunk said: 'In, you may go out now to play again with Out.' After a while, Out started misbehaving, so the mother skunk shouted: 'Out you come in and In you stay out.' A little later, just as it was starting to get dark, she said: 'Out you go out and bring In back with you.' The mother skunk was very surprised when, after only a few minutes, Out returned with In. 'How did you find In so quickly?' she asked. 'It was easy,' Out replied, 'In stinked!'

☺ • ☺ • ☺

WAY OUT IN the Mid-West, two horses were talking to each other outside a saloon bar. 'I was out on the prairie the other day, rounding up some buffalo, when, all of a sudden, a flash of lightning appeared and I threw my rider,' one was telling the other. 'Funny you should say that,' said the other, 'Exactly the same happened to me, when my owner took me out there was a sudden flash of lightning and I threw him into a pond.' Just at that moment, a donkey, tied up on the same rail, looked up and said: 'Isn't that amazing. I was coming out of the stable with my owner when a blinding flash startled me and I ran into a gate, throwing him over the gate and into a ditch.' 'I can't believe I'm hearing this,' said one of the horses. 'What's that?' said the other. 'A donkey talking, he must be some sort of an ass.'

☺ • ☺ • ☺

WE INTERRUPT THIS radio programme to bring you an urgent news flash: a jumbo jet has just been hijacked by a cat, which is demanding it be taken to the Canaries!"

A GORILLA WALKS into this saloon bar and orders a beer. 'That'll be 50 dollars,' said the barman. The gorilla drank the beer and asked for another. 'That'll be 50 dollars,' said the barman. After finishing his second drink, the gorilla asked for a third. 'Certainly, sir. That'll be another 50 dollars. You know,' continued the barman, 'we don't get many gorillas in this bar.' 'I'm not surprised,' replied the gorilla, 'at those prices.'

☺ ● ☺ ● ☺

THIS STORY MAY sound a little fishy, but this prawn swam home one day and said to her Mum: 'I'm going to marry a crab.' 'Marry a crab!' the mother prawn said, 'You can't marry a crab. For one thing, they walk sideways.' 'Actually,' said the lovestruck young prawn, 'he came in last night walking perfectly straight.' The mother prawn wasn't impressed. 'That's only because he'd had too much to drink!'

☺ ● ☺ ● ☺

A GUY TOOK his pet monkey into this saloon bar for a drink. After a few drinks, the monkey dropped dead. The man decided to leave but, just as he was walking out of the bar, the barman shouted after him: 'You can't leave that lyin' there!' 'It's not a lion,' the man called back, 'it's a monkey!'

☺ ● ☺ ● ☺

A DAIRY FARMER, whose cows had frozen up called at his next door neighbour's farm. 'I hear your cows froze up last week,' he said. 'That's right,' his neighbour replied. 'Well, now my cows have frozen up too and I was wondering how you thawed your cows out.' 'Simple. I called our new veterinary surgeon in. She's really good at her job. She only had to touch all the cows and they were defrosted.' 'Will you give me her telephone number? Oh, and by the way, what's her name?' 'Thora Herd!'

ANIMAL CRACKERS 13

A GUY WALKS into his local dog kennels and asks: 'Have you any dogs for sale?' 'Yes,' replies the owner, 'What breed would you like?' 'I don't mind so much about the breed as long as the dog is black and white.' 'Black and white,' says the owner, rather surprised, 'why's that?' 'Well, you see the black and white licence is so much cheaper.'

☺ • ☺ • ☺

THIS SNAIL WON the National Lottery and went straight round to buy a fabulous Rolls Royce. 'Will you spray a very big 'S' on the back of my new Rolls?' he asked the salesman. 'A big 'S', replied the salesman, 'Why?' 'So you can watch this 'S' car go!' said the snail.

☺ • ☺ • ☺

A MAN SENT for the veterinary surgeon to come round and give his pets a check up. 'Now, Sir, what pets have you got?' asked the vet. 'I've got a dog, a cat and a newt,' the man replied. 'Fine,' said the vet, 'I'll examine your dog first. By the way what's his name?' 'Patch.' 'Why do you call him Patch.' 'Well, because he's got a black patch over his eye.' The vet examined the dog and passed him fit. 'Now I'll take a look at your cat. What's his name?' 'I call him Ginger.' 'Why's that?' 'Because he's got a ginger coat.' The vet checked the cat and he was fine as well. 'Now, how about your newt? What's his name?' 'Tiny.' 'Why Tiny?' 'Well, because he's minute.'

☺ • ☺ • ☺

A PELICAN STROLLED into this bar and asked the barman: 'Can I have a bottle of beer please, Budweiser preferably?' 'Certainly,' replied the barman opening up the bottle of Budweiser, 'are you paying for it now?' 'No,' said the pelican, 'will you put it on my bill?'

WAY OUT IN the mid-West, a three-legged dog staggered into a saloon bar, went up to the bar and ordered a drink. The barman served him and then asked: 'What you are doing out here?' 'Well,' said the dog, 'I'se a lookin' for the man who shot my paw!'

☺ ● ☺ ● ☺

TWO NEXT-DOOR neighbours out in the country both kept bees. The odd thing was that while one of them had loads and loads of honey, the other had none. So one day the one who had no honey, popped his head over the hedgerow and asked his neighbour: 'How is it you only live next door to me, and yet your bees produce loads of honey and mine hardly any?' 'Well,' the neighbour replied, 'you don't treat your bees right!' 'How do you mean?' 'I get up early in the morning and let my bees out. They fly over into the park to get at all the fresh flowers and then they return laden with pollen so they can produce loads of honey.' 'Thanks!' he said, rushing inside to tell his wife. 'It's no wonder we don't get any honey,' he told her, 'we're doing it all wrong. The guy next door gets up at 6 o'clock in the morning and lets his bees out early so they can go into the park to get at all the fresh new flowers.' 'Don't take any notice of him,' she replied, 'he's telling you a pack of lies. The park doesn't open until 9 am.'

☺ ● ☺ ● ☺

TWO FOREST RANGERS were patrolling in a National State Park when they came across an elephant stuck on a branch at the top of a tree. 'How are we going to get him down?' asked one of the rangers. 'Easy,' said the other, 'tell him to crawl onto a leaf and then wait until the Fall.'

☺ ● ☺ ● ☺

TWO FLEAS WERE playing football in a saucer. 'We're not playing very well are we?' one flea said to the other. 'No,' said the other flea, 'and we'd better improve by the weekend.' 'Why's that?' 'Because we're playing in the cup next Saturday!'

ANIMAL CRACKERS

A GUY WAS sitting alone in a club one night with not a penny to spend, when he suddenly had an idea. He approached the owner of the club and asked him: 'If I get up and entertain the people would you give me a drink?' The owner of the club replied: 'If you get this crowd going you can have a meal and a drink.' The guy disappeared outside and came back a few minutes later with a bulldog. He sat the dog down at the piano and told it start playing. This brought the audience to its feet, clapping and cheering. 'Well done!' said the delighted owner, 'here's your meal and a drink.'

A little while later, the guy had another idea. 'If I get you a really good singer,' he asked the owner, 'will you give me a week's accommodation?' 'Sure,' the owner replied, 'if you can get this crowd going even more you're on.' The guy vanished again and returned with a budgie. Placing the bird on the lid of the piano, he again asked the bulldog to play. As he did the budgie started singing, bringing the audience once more to its feet with rapturous applause. 'Well,' said the owner, 'you've certainly earned that week's accommodation.'

Just then, a theatrical agent, who happened to be in the audience, came up and asked the guy: 'How much do you want for the budgie?' 'Oh, I'm afraid he's not for sale,' he replied. The agent tried again. 'If I pay you £1,000 in cash, will you sell me the bird?' 'OK,' the guy replied, 'its a deal.' The agent paid up and took the bird with him.

When he left, the owner of the club turned to the guy and said: 'That was stupid. A bird that can sing like that is worth much more than £1,000!' 'Oh no,' said the guy, 'it doesn't really sing. You see, the bulldog's a ventriloquist.'

☺ • ☺ • ☺

ONE DAY A guy was waiting at a bus stop holding onto a penguin. The next guy in the queue turned round to him and said: 'That penguin should be in a zoo where it can be near water.' 'I know,' replied the guy with the penguin, 'that's where I'm taking him.' The next day the same two guys were waiting at the same bus stop and this guy was still holding onto the penguin. 'I thought you were taking that penguin to the zoo,' the other guy said. 'Oh, I did that yesterday,' replied the first guy, 'Today I'm taking him to the cinema.'

MEDICAL MEN

A YOUNG MOTHER took her daughter to the doctor's as she didn't seem very well. After a thorough examination, the doctor told the mother: 'I'm afraid your daughter's pregnant.' 'You must be out of your mind!' the mother exclaimed, 'My daughter's never so much as kissed a man, have you pet?' 'No, Mum,' came the reply, 'I haven't even held a man's hand.' The doctor jumped up out of his chair, ran over to the window and gazed very intently at the sky. A long silence prevailed until the mother asked: 'Is there something wrong out there, doctor?' 'Not at all,' he replied, 'only the last time this occurred, a strange star appeared in the East, and I don't want to miss it this time!'

MEDICAL MEN

THIS GUY GOES to see his doctor. 'One minute I keep thinking I'm a teepee,' he tells him, 'and then the next, I think I'm a wigwam.' 'Ah,' explained the doctor, 'I know what's wrong with you. You're too tents!'

☺ ● ☺ ● ☺

A MAN WENT to see his doctor. 'How can I help you?' the doctor asked. 'Well you see, doctor, I have pains all over my body,' the man replied. 'Where exactly?' asked the doctor, 'Will you show me?' 'Everywhere I touch with my finger.' The patient started touching all over body saying, 'There, there, and there.' 'Right,' said the doctor, 'sit down and I'll examine you.' After he'd finished, he declared: 'Its clear what's wrong with you. You've got a broken finger.'

☺ ● ☺ ● ☺

A GUY GOES to the doctor. 'I keep thinking I'm a dog,' he tells him. 'That's strange. I'll have to give you a thorough examination, will you please get up on the couch.' 'Oh, I'm sorry doctor,' replied the patient, 'but I'm not allowed on the couch!'

☺ ● ☺ ● ☺

THIS GUY GOES to his doctor's surgery one day. 'I have a problem,' he explains, 'I keep hallucinating. One minute I think I'm a bell, then another minute I think I'm a bumble bee.' After giving the man a thorough examination, the doctor says: 'At this moment in time, you appear to be stable, however, I'm going to prescribe some tablets which I want you to take right away. When you've completed the course you should be all right, but if for any reason this problem should recur, please don't hesitate to give me a ring or a buzz.'

☺ ● ☺ ● ☺

A GUY WENT to see his doctor. 'I've a most peculiar problem,' he tells him, 'I keep thinking I'm a pair of curtains.' 'Then I'm afraid,' said the doctor, 'all I can say is that you'll have to pull yourself together.'

NEXT APPLICANT PLEASE!

THREE GUYS TURNED up for a job interview. The manager called the first applicant into his office. 'I want to make this interview quick and easy,' he told him, 'to find out who is the most observant out of the three of you. I want you to look at me and say if you can detect any faults on me.' The applicant looked at the manager all over and then said: 'Yes, I have spotted a fault. You've got one ear higher than the other.' 'Excellent!' said the manager, 'send the next applicant in.' He repeated the procedure, and the second applicant, having looked him all over, said: 'You've got one ear lower than the other.' 'Magnificent!' said the manager, 'send the final applicant in.' The third applicant came in and the manager asked him to find the fault. Having examined him from head to toe, he said, 'I've spotted the fault! You wear contact lenses.' 'That,' said the manager, 'is the most intelligent and observant answer I've heard all day, you've got the job. But tell me, how on earth did you detect that I wore contact lenses?' 'Well, sir,' he said, 'there's no way you could wear glasses with ears like that!'

NEXT APPLICANT PLEASE 19

TWO GUYS APPLIED to become detectives so they turned up at their local police station for an interview. One of them was sitting nervously outside when his friend came out from his interview. 'How did you get on?' he asked him. 'Fine,' his friend replied, 'I've got the job. In fact, I've been given my first case.' 'What's that?' 'Who killed Cock Robin.'

☺ ● ☺ ● ☺

A GUY WENT for a job interview and was called into the boss's office. 'I'm going to ask you one simple question and if your answer is good enough you'll get the job' he said. 'The question is: What is the definition of fascinate?' The applicant thought very deeply and then, all of a sudden, replied: 'it's curious.' 'Curious!' said the boss, 'How do you come by that answer?' 'Well,' said the applicant, 'I've just been given an overcoat as a present and, as it's been very cold recently, I've been wearing it a lot. The coat has ten buttons, but I'm very curious why I can only fasten eight!'

☺ ● ☺ ● ☺

DURING A JOB interview the applicant was asked 'Can you define a Scouser?' 'Yes,' he replied, 'its someone who lives in Liverpool, England. He sets off for work in the morning, shouts down the Mersey Tunnel which connects Liverpool and Birkenhead under the River Mersey, and picks up the Echo on his way home from work at night.'

☺ ● ☺ ● ☺

BRUSHES WITH THE LAW

THE POLICE WERE called to a disturbance outside a zoo. When they arrived they found a guy shouting angrily at the pay kiosk. They arrested him and drove him down to the police station where he was sat in an interview room. 'Why did you make such a nuisance of yourself?' asked the police officer. 'Well,' the man replied, 'I was originally inside the zoo but they threw me out.' 'Why did they do that?' 'Because I wanted to go into the lions' cage.' 'Why did you want to do that?' 'Well, you see, I love line dancing'

☺ ● ☺ ● ☺

POLICE RUSHED TO a bank where a robbery had just taken place. The detective asked the teller: 'What was the robber wearing?' 'He was dressed as a gorilla,' replied the teller. 'Would you recognise him again?' 'I doubt it, he had a mask on!'

BRUSHES WITH THE LAW

A DOCKER ON his way home from work one night was just passing the security gate window. Suddenly the security guard rushed out and demanded of the startled docker: 'What did you stamp your foot on outside my window?' 'Only a snail,' the docker replied. 'What did you do that for?' 'Well, because it's been following me around all day!'

☺ ● ☺ ● ☺

A MAN WAS driving his horse and cart along the road when, all of a sudden, his horse dropped dead. He rushed up to report the accident to a policeman. 'Where did this happen?' the policeman asked. 'In Conduit Street.' 'Can you spell it?' 'No, I can't, but never mind, I'll drag the horse round the corner to Bond Street, I can spell that!'

☺ ● ☺ ● ☺

A DOCKER HAD just finished work for the day and was on his way home carrying a large bale of cotton on his shoulder. As he passed the gate he was stopped by the security guard who asked him: 'Where are you going with that bale of cotton?' 'Home,' replied the docker, 'I've got a terrible earache!'

☺ ● ☺ ● ☺

A MATTER OF TASTE

A GUY SAW a sign outside a burger bar which said, TRY OUR BRAND NEW BURGER! So in he went to buy one of the new burgers. It was huge, with layers of beef, cheese, tomatoes, onions, and mushrooms, all coated with tomato sauce. He got it to his table and, with great difficulty, picked it up and took a bite, only to have its contents spilling out all over his clothes. He stood up and, while holding the burger at shoulder height away from his clothes with his left hand, started brushing off the tomato sauce and burger bits. An assistant rushed up. 'Can I help you, sir?' he enquired apologetically, 'This keeps on happening, ever since we brought out the new burger.' 'By the way,' asked the guy, 'what's the new burger called?' 'A banjo burger.' 'Why's that?' 'Well, after seeing everyone brushing their right hand up and down, what better name!'

A MATTER OF TASTE

A CANNIBAL TRIBE once captured an explorer and took him back to their village. Their chief ordered them to place him whole into a big cooking pot together with all the vegetables. 'I'll be back in one hour,' he told them. An hour later, he returned to the village only to see the big cooking pot over the fire being stirred with a big stick and the explorer's head floating around in it. The chief was angry. 'I told you to cook him slowly in one piece! Why did you cut his head off?' The cannibal stirring the pot explained: 'We had to. He was eating all the potatoes.'

☺ ● ☺ ● ☺

A GUY WALKS into his local Pizza Hut. He goes up the counter and orders a pizza to take away. 'Would you like the pizza cut up into eight or 16 pieces?' asks the girl behind the counter. 'Eight pieces please,' the guy replies, 'there's no way I could eat sixteen.'

☺ ● ☺ ● ☺

A MAN INVENTED a new type of cheese so he went to a large cheese distributor in order to get it onto the market. He met the managing director of the company and excitedly told him about his new cheese. 'What's it called?' asked the MD. 'I've decided to call it Cheshire Cheese!' 'But we already have Cheshire Cheese!' replied the MD. 'What about Lancashire?' 'We already have that as well!' 'How about Cheddar?' 'That, too!' 'Edam?' 'I'm sorry. You'll have to go away and think of a new name.' Three weeks later, the man returned to the cheese company. 'I've found a unique name for my new cheese.' 'What's that then?' asked the MD. 'Well, I've just come back from the Middle East so I've decided to call it Cheeses of Nazareth!'

TWO HUNGRY CANNIBALS captured a lone explorer in the jungle. As they walked back to the village, one of them asked the explorer who he was and where he came from. 'I'm on vacation and decided to do a little exploring. To be honest, I'm actually a very famous comedian.' Later that evening, as the two cannibals tucked into the famous – now former – entertainer, the cannibal said to his friend: 'He was right, this meat tastes funny!'

DEMON DRINK

TWO FRIENDS WERE having a drink in a bar when, all of a sudden, one of them burst out laughing. The other one asked him what he was laughing at, and he replied: 'Haven't you seen that guy at the other end of the bar, he's got a flat head.' 'You shouldn't laugh at that,' said his friend, 'He's a very brave guy. He propped up the wood support down in a mine shaft when it started collapsing and saved many miners lives.' 'Oh, I see. Sorry, I didn't know.' They carried on drinking for a while and then he suddenly burst out laughing again. 'What is it now?' said his friend. 'It's that guy with the flat head, I've just noticed he's got a flat sideface as well.' 'You shouldn't laugh at that either.' 'Why's that?' 'Well, they had to knock him into place with a shovel to support the pitshaft roof!'

TWO PLAYERS WERE having a game of snooker in a club when, all of a sudden, one of the players asked: 'Have you seen that girl on the next table? She's potting every ball in sight and playing a load of trick shots while balancing a glass of beer on her head at the same time.' The other player replied: 'Don't you know who that is? That's Beer Tricks Potter.'

☺ • ☺ • ☺

A GUY WALKED into a saloon bar. 'Would you like a drink, Sir?' asked the barman. 'Oh, thank you,' he replied. 'I'll have a large beer.' The barman handed him his drink and waited a few minutes before asking him: 'Aren't you going to pay for it?' 'Certainly not!' the guy retorted, 'you asked me when I walked in: "Would you like a drink?" so I'm certainly not paying for it.' A lawyer, who happened to be standing at the bar and had heard the conversation, told the barman: 'The customer's quite within his rights not to pay because you asked him when he walked into the bar: "Would you like a drink?" This maddened the barman, who turned to the guy who'd had the free drink and told him: 'Right! As soon as you finish that drink, get out and don't come back, you're barred!' So the guy supped up and vanished, but the following week he returned. The same barman was on duty and as soon as he saw the guy walk in he shouted: 'I told you last week, you're barred, so get out!' 'Barred?' the guy protested, 'But I've never been in here before in my life!' 'Are you sure you've never been in here before?' asked the barman, suddenly unsure of himself. 'Absolutely certain.' 'In that case, I'm very sorry sir. You know, you must have a double.' 'Thank you very much,' said the guy, 'I'll have a Double Brandy!'

☺ • ☺ • ☺

A WORKMAN WAS busy laying Tarmac on a very hot day, so he decided to dive into a nearby pub for a refreshing glass of beer. When he'd finished his drink, he asked the barman: 'Would it be alright if I take another beer out with me?' 'Certainly, you can,' replied the barman, 'but its so hot, why do you want to take it outside?' 'Well,' the workman explained, 'it's one for the road!'

NIGHT CLUBBING

A GUY WAS just about to walk into a night club when he was stopped by the doorman. 'You can't come in tonight, it's fancy dress only,' he said. 'But I *am* in fancy dress,' said the guy. 'What are you supposed to be?' asked the doorman. 'I'm a turtle.' 'If you're a turtle then what's that girl doing on your back.' The guy immediately replied: 'Oh, that's Michelle!'

☺ ● ☺ ● ☺

A YOUNG GIRL went to a nightclub looking forward to a long night's dancing. She went to the cloakroom to leave her coat but was struck by the handsome young cloakroom attendant. She was so taken with him that she spent the entire evening in conversation with him. As she was about to leave she said: 'By the way, I didn't ask you your name, or where you came from?' 'Well,' he replied, 'I come from Scotland and my name is Angus McCoatup!'

A VERY PRETTY young girl was about to walk into a night club when she was stopped at the door by the bouncer. 'Where are you going?' he asked her. 'To the Disco.' she replied. 'But what's that you're holding in your hand?' 'Oh, it's a mushroom.' 'A mushroom!' the doorman exclaimed, 'Why are you taking a mushroom into the club?' 'Because he's a hell of a fungi to be out with!'

☺ ● ☺ ● ☺

ONE NIGHT AT a club a big row developed between two rival gangs and they started fighting. The bouncer calmly walked over to the brawling youngsters and sprayed them all with an aerosol can. All of a sudden, the fighting stopped and the two gangs started laughing, joking and shaking hands with each other. The manager of the club was very impressed so he went up to the bouncer and asked: 'How did you do that?' 'Easy,' he replied, 'I sprayed them all with Harmony hair spray!'

☺ ● ☺ ● ☺

THE OPEN ROAD

THREE FRIENDS WERE taking their four-wheel drive through the Sahara Desert, when suddenly the engine cut out. As hard as they tried, they couldn't get it to start so they decided to abandon it and continue on foot. Two of them started walking, looking round only to see their friend still standing by the car. 'Come on,' they called to him. 'Wait a minute!' he replied, 'I'm taking the car radiator with me.' 'Why are you doing that?' they asked. 'Well, if I get dehydrated, I can drink the water from the radiator.' 'In that case,' said the second friend, 'I'm taking the wheel caps and if it gets really hot, I can put them over my head to keep the sun off.' The third man thought for a minute and then wrenched off the door. 'If it gets that hot,' he told them, 'I can wind the window down!'

THREE GIRLS WERE out on a drive together enjoying the beautiful countryside when suddenly a hare leapt out in front of their car and was run over. The girl who was driving was really upset. She jumped out of the car, picked the hare up and carried it to the side of the road. 'You can't leave it there,' said one of the other girls, 'it might roll back down onto the road.' So off the driver went to put the hare down in the woods. On returning to the car, her friends asked her: 'What on earth did you do to that hare? It's waving at you like mad from the edge of the forest.' 'Oh, nothing really,' she replied, 'I just sprayed it with my permanent wave hair restorer.'

☺ ● ☺ ● ☺

A GUY OWNED a Datsun car which was his pride and joy. He'd had it many years and had lavished hours of care on it. In return he'd enjoyed years of trouble-free driving. Then, one day, his gearbox failed. He went to his local Datsun agent, who told him that he was in need of parts from Japan, but first had to find someone to go and collect a plane-load of Datsun gearbox parts. 'That's fine,' said the man, 'I'll go.' A few days later he was jetting of to Japan to pick up the parts. On the return journey, however, as the plane was passing over the Sahara Desert, the pilot suddenly announced: 'I'm afraid we're having trouble with one of our four engines and I've had to shut it down, which means that we'll have to jettison all the cargo in the hold into the desert.' At that moment, two Arabs were happily riding their camels in the desert below, one of them looked up into the sky and shouted to his friend: 'Look it's raining Datsun cogs!'

☺ ● ☺ ● ☺

A FARMER WON the lottery. He was so excited that he dashed down to his local car showroom without even changing out of his working clothes. He bought himself a brand new sports car, but after an hour on the road, he phoned up the showroom. 'This car you've just sold me,' he complained, 'you told me it would do 120 miles an hour.' 'That's correct sir!' 'Well I'm afraid you're wrong, I can only get it up to 25 miles an hour.' 'Tell me, sir, what gear are you in?' 'I'm wearing an old hat and Wellington boots.'

THE OPEN ROAD

A FARMER WAS enjoying a well-earned drink in his local pub, still wearing his working gear of green Wellington boots and flat cap. He was just about to take a swig of his beer when he heard a loud voice coming from the far end of the bar. 'I own a Porsche which will do 150 miles an hour without any trouble,' said the voice. 'Wow!' said all the other men standing around the bar.

All of a sudden, the farmer looked up and shouted down the bar: 'Did I hear you say you had a Porsche that'll do 150 miles an hour?' 'Yes,' said the Porsche owner. 'Well, I can do that speed.' 'What car have you got?' 'I haven't got a car, I just run fast, I challenge you to a race.' All the customers started placed bets on the race of the century, and the pub's landlord went out to give them a chequered flag start.

Off they both zoomed, with the farmer running alongside the Porsche. The Porsche driver increased his speed to 100 miles an hour, only to see the farmer still keeping up with him. He jammed his foot down hard on the throttle. He was now doing 150 miles an hour, but as he looked across he could still see the farmer running alongside.

Suddenly, the farmer took off and vanished out of sight. The Porsche driver, angry at being beaten, kept his foot down, but when he came to a very sharp left hand bend where a large crowd had gathered, he slammed his brakes on.

As he jumped out of his Porsche he asked a man in the crowd: 'What's happening?' 'You'll never believe this,' he replied, 'a guy running at terrific speed overtook a Porsche – he must have been doing about 180 miles a hour – when all of a sudden, in the middle of the bend, he had a blowout in his left Wellington boot!'

☺ • ☺ • ☺

A GUY WON the lottery so he took himself down to his local car showroom and bought himself a brand new car. Leaving the showroom, he decided to take his new car out for a spin. After an hour on the open road, he took the car back, very upset. 'Is there a problem?' the salesman asked him. 'There certainly is! You told me that this car can get up to 100.' 'Yes, that's right sir.' 'Well, I live on a very steep hill at number 96 and I couldn't even get it up to 90!'

THE PROUD OWNER of a Rolls Royce was casually driving along a quiet country lane, enjoying the beautiful scenery, when he spotted a guy walking along the road with his dog. All of a sudden, there was a rumble of thunder followed by a shower of torrential rain. The driver pulled up alongside the guy and wound down the window. 'Can I help you?' he asked. 'That's very kind of you. Actually, I've just run out of petrol and I was walking down to next service station.' 'Well, hop in, but would you mind not bringing your dog in, he's so wet he'll ruin my carpets.' 'That's OK, he can run alongside.' The guy got in the car and the two set off for the petrol station. Soon they were cruising along at 80 miles an hour when the driver suddenly remembered the dog. He slammed his foot down on the brake. 'Where's your dog now?' he asked his passenger. 'Oh, don't worry about him,' he replied, 'he's still outside.' The driver looked out of the window and was astonished to see the dog standing there, having pulled up alongside the car. 'What a fantastic dog,' he said, 'but what's that roll of fur stuck on his head?' 'Oh, that's his tail,' said the dog's owner, 'he's never pulled up so quickly before!'

☺ ● ☺ ● ☺

ALL AT SEA

A GUY SET sail on a cruise around the Middle Eastern ports. He was walking around the upper deck, finding his sailing feet, so to speak, when all of a sudden he realised he needed the toilet. He hastily approached a steward who was walking around the deck. 'Excuse me, could you direct me to the nearest toilet?' he asked him. 'Certainly, sir, it's port side.' 'Port Said!' exclaimed the passenger, 'I can't wait until I get *there*!'

☺ ● ☺ ● ☺

A NAVAL DIVER swimming along the sea-bed came across a very sick octopus. Feeling sorry for the octopus, he decided to take it aboard the ship up above. When he surfaced next to the ship, he called up: 'Is the medical officer on board?' 'Yes,' they replied. 'Then will you go and get him' When the medical officer arrived, the diver threw the octopus onto the deck and shouted: 'That's the sick squid I owe you!'

A MAN WAS given a beautiful fishing rod for his birthday, so he decided to go deep sea fishing with it. When he was well out at sea, he cast his line. Almost immediately he got a bite. He tried to reel in his catch, but realised he couldn't, as the catch was so heavy that it was bending his new rod. He didn't want to break the rod so he decided to reel out his line, but the catch was so heavy he eventually ran out of line. Rather than lose his rod altogether, he held tightly onto it only to end up hurtling through the water at a terrific speed towards the jaws of this huge whale, which swallowed him whole. He started swimming around inside the whale, only to hear the sound of people singing, so he swam towards the sound, only to find four guys sitting on a plank singing their heads off. 'Hello there!' he called, 'How do you get out of here?' 'No way, it's impossible,' they replied. 'Then how is it you're all singing so happily?' the man asked. 'Oh,' they replied, 'everyone sings in whales!'

☺ • ☺ • ☺

TWO GUYS APPLIED for jobs as barmen on a cruise ship and were told to report to the Purser on board. 'Right,' he told them, 'One of you can operate the bar on 'A' Deck and the other, the one on 'B' Deck.' Shortly after the ship had set sail the two men opened up their bars. After quite a while, the guy on 'B' Deck hadn't had a single customer. Thinking that the guy on 'A' Deck had taken all his customers away, he proceeded up to 'A' Deck where he found the other barman also without any customers. 'Where have they all gone?' asked the 'B' deck barman. 'I don't really know,' said the 'A' Deck barman, 'The only thing I can think is they've all gone to the dance.' 'The dance?' said the 'B' Deck barman, 'What dance is that?' 'Well, didn't you hear the announcement about half an hour ago?' 'No. What was it?' 'A band on ship!'

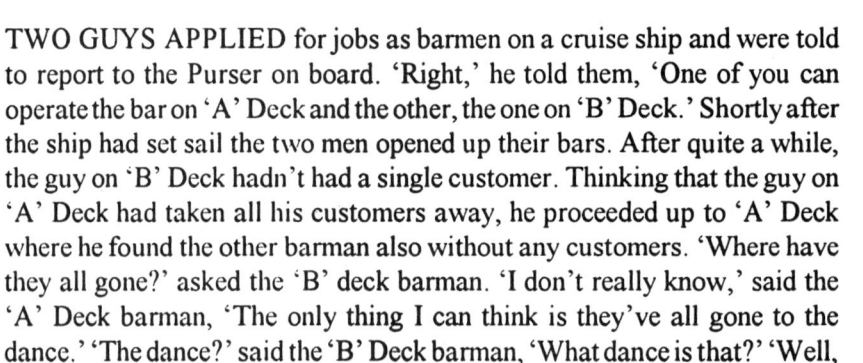

☺ • ☺ • ☺

ON A WING AND A PRAYER

THE PILOT OF a light aircraft was flying over a town, when suddenly his engine cut out. After desperate efforts to restart the engine, he decided the only alternative was to bale out. After jumping and clearing the aircraft, he pulled the ripcord to open his parachute, but it wouldn't operate. Hurtling down to earth at tremendous speed, he was astonished to see a guy zooming up towards him on a gas stove. The pilot shouted: 'Do you know anything about parachutes?' 'No,' the man called back, 'do you know anything about gas stoves?'

TWO ASTRONAUTS WERE being interviewed on television before takeoff. 'Where are you going to?' they were asked. 'We're going to the Sun,' they replied. 'The Sun!' exclaimed the reporter, 'Won't you get burnt up before you get there?' 'Oh no,' said the Astronauts, 'we're going by night.'

☺ • ☺ • ☺

SUDDENLY, DURING A long airline flight, the flight navigator turned to the pilot and said: 'My computer's gone down and I've no idea where we are.' 'Don't worry,' said the pilot, winding down the window in his cockpit and stretching his arm outside, 'we're over the North Pole.' 'How do you know that?' asked the navigator. 'Because my hand has snow and ice on it.' 'Well,' said the navigator, 'that means we're going in the wrong direction. We'll have to do a 'U' turn.' So the pilot did a U-turn. Four hours later, the navigator came up to him and asked: 'Where are we now?' Once again, the pilot wound down the window and stuck his arm outside. 'We're over the Sahara Desert,' he said. 'How do you know?' 'Because my hand is red hot and has sand all over it.' Then we'll have to do another 'U' turn because we're going in the wrong direction again.' After another four hours, the navigator said to the pilot: 'I'm really worried now, if we're not over our destination right now we're in trouble as we're nearly out of fuel.' The pilot wound his window down and put his arm out. 'Don't worry,' he said, 'we're spot on!' 'Spot on. How do you know?' 'Easy, someone's just stolen my watch.'

☺ • ☺ • ☺

HOME FROM HOME

A TOURIST SPENT the night at a small hotel. Next morning, he got up out of bed, took a shower, and went down for breakfast. The landlady served him a hearty breakfast of eggs, bacon, sausages, mushrooms and tomatoes. The guest looked at the plate and said: 'That looks lovely, but the only trouble is, I don't eat that kind of breakfast.' 'Oh, I see,' replied the landlady, 'Well, what *do* you eat?' 'I only eat Baked Beans.' 'Fine,' she said, disappearing into the kitchen, 'I'll be back shortly.' When she returned she was carrying a very large plate piled high with Baked Beans. The guest thanked her and tucked in, leaving his plate clean. After returning briefly to his room to pack, he settled up with the landlady and went on his way. Two hours later, a policeman knocked at the door of the hotel with a photograph of the tourist. 'Did this gentleman stay here last night?' he asked the landlady. 'Yes, why?' 'Well, I'm sorry to say he's just jumped off the Town Hall roof.' 'I can't believe it!' gasped the landlady, 'Why would he do that?' 'He must have been depressed,' the policeman replied. 'Oh no, officer, there's no way that guy was depressed. When he left here this morning, he was full of beans.'

THREE GUYS WERE travelling through the Mojave Desert, when suddenly they were captured by Indians. The Indian Chief told them 'We are going to kill you one by one with our arrows. However, we are a very understanding and thoughtful tribe, so we always grant our prisoners a last request.' The three guys tossed a coin to see who would go first. The first one to go told the chief: 'I'd like a bottle of Scotch.' After finishing the Scotch, he threw the bottle into the sand. The Indians fired the arrows at him and he dropped to the ground. The second guy asked the Chief for a very large cigar, thinking it would last longer. After a long time, and still trying to hold on to the cigar until it burnt his fingers, he had to drop it in the sand. All the arrows hit him and he, too, fell to the ground. The third guy said: 'I'd like some aftershave.' 'Aftershave?' said the Chief. 'Well, if that's your request, you can have it.' The guy splashed the aftershave all over himself and threw away the bottle. The Indians fired at him, but not one arrow hit. 'I can't believe this,' declared the Chief, 'but it's fate and you can go free, but first, tell me how was it that not one arrow hit you?' 'Well, you see, its my aftershave,' the guy explained, 'it's called Arrow-miss!'

☺ • ☺ • ☺

A GUY ON vacation in a beautiful village was enjoying a drink in a lovely old country pub when he was astonished to see all these lovely girls running past him with no clothes on. A few minutes later a load of men, also with no clothes on, rushed past wooing the girls ahead of them. The guy asked the landlord of the pub what was going on. 'It's our fertility week,' he explained, 'and all the girls run up into the hills and into all different caves, followed by the men trying to woo them.' 'Can I join in?' asked the guy. 'Certainly, but I would wait until tomorrow and follow them up then.' The following evening, the guy was waiting outside the pub, raring to go. First the girls ran by, then the men, and off he went up the hill. He raced into the first cave he came to, wooing like mad, but he heard no reply. So he carried on deeper into the cave, still wooing, when at last he heard 'woo .... woo....' and was run over by a train!

HOME FROM HOME

TWO EXPLORERS WERE trekking through the dense jungle when they came upon a wide clearing with very high grass. Suddenly they were startled to see a tribe of natives jumping up and down in the long grass. One explorer turned to the other and said: 'I wonder what tribe they are?' 'They're the Hellarwe tribe,' his friend replied. 'How do you know?' 'Didn't you hear when they were jumping up and down they were all shouting: "Where the hell are we?"'

☺ • ☺ • ☺

A YOUNG CHINESE girl, backpacking around the World, found herself staying at this tiny hotel in a picturesque village in Europe. She made great friends with the owners and, during one of their many conversations, she asked them about their children. 'Well,' the owner explained, rather sadly, 'we've a daughter in London but she never writes to us.' 'Don't worry,' said the girl, 'London's my next destination. Where will I find her?' 'Well, the last we heard, she was in W.C.1' 'What's her name?' 'Neary Dunn.' Soon after arriving in London, the backpacker needed to go to the toilet, only to be confronted with a sign over the door which read 'W.C.' Knocking on the door, she asked, 'Are you Neary Dunn?' 'Yes.' came the reply. 'Well, don't you think you should write home to your Mum and Dad?'

☺ • ☺ • ☺

A GUY WAS on vacation when he drove into this beautiful town and decided it would be a lovely place to look around and spend the night. He began searching for a place to stay and saw a small hotel with a notice which read: BED, BREAKFAST AND EVENING MEAL, EN-SUITE WITH BATH. He went in and asked the girl behind the desk: 'Can you give me bed and breakfast with a bath?' 'I can give you bed and breakfast,' she replied, 'but you'll have to take the bath yourself!'

A HOLIDAYING AMERICAN was touring the English countryside when he stopped at a five-barred gate to view the land. As he was leaning over the gate, a farmer drove up behind the wheel of his tractor. 'Tell me, sir,' the tourist asked him, 'how far does your land stretch?' 'See those hills in the distance and the forest to the right?' replied the farmer. 'Well that's my land.' The American wasn't impressed. 'You know,' he said, 'way back home, I have a ranch and in the morning I can get into my car and two days later I'm still on my own land.' 'Aye,' said the farmer, 'I had a car like that once!'

☺ ● ☺ ● ☺

A JOURNALIST WAS on holiday, sightseeing amongst the Red Indian reservations. He drove into a well-known tribe's camp and asked for an interview with the Big Chief, Running Water. As he entered the Chief's wigwam, he bowed and said: 'Hello, Big Chief Running Water, thank you for allowing to meet and talk with you. I work for a newspaper and would like to write a column about you.' After conducting a lengthy interview with the Chief, the reporter asked: 'I've heard that you're famous for your amazing memory. Could you tell me what you had for breakfast on Christmas Day in the year 1930?' Immediately, the Chief replied: 'Eggs.' The reporter thanked the Chief and left. About ten years later, he found himself again on vacation in the same area, so he decided to call in on Big Chief Running Water. He thought it would be a nice gesture to greet him in his own language so, as he entered the wigwam, he said to the Big Chief: 'How!' The Chief looked up and replied: 'Scrambled.'

☺ ● ☺ ● ☺

EARLY ONE MORNING, the refuse men were collecting and emptying the bins, when they came to a house with no bin outside. One of the refuse men knocked on the door and a man appeared. 'Where's ya bin?,' he asked. 'I'se bin to Hong Kong!' the man replied. 'No. Where's ya Wheelie Bin?' 'I'se weally bin to Hong Kong!'

FANCY THAT!

ONE DAY, AN old lady was busy dusting, when she came upon this very old lamp which she started polishing very hard. All of a sudden, a genie appeared out of the lamp. The genie said to the old lady: 'You have three wishes, what are they?' The old lady, startled, flabbergasted and pleased, said: 'Well, first, I'd like to be very young and attractive; second, I'd like to be very rich; and third, I'd like my pet cat to be my young lover.' 'Your wishes are my command,' said the genie. There was a flash and suddenly the old lady turned into a beautiful young woman. Another flash, and out of the sky poured sackloads of money Then, another big flash, the cat vanished and a very young, attractive man appeared in its place. He was looking very upset. 'What's the matter?' the, now beautiful and young, woman asked the handsome young man. 'Well,' he replied, 'did you have to have me castrated?'

A MAN WAS about to go into the Job Centre to sign on, when he met an old friend outside who warned him: 'Be careful what you say in there, they're finding jobs for everyone today.' Once inside the man went up to the clerk behind the counter and said: 'I'd like to sign on.' 'Just a minute,' said the clerk, 'I might have a job for you. What's your occupation?' 'I'm a professional Ballet Dancer.' 'Oh, sorry sir,' said the clerk after checking his list, 'we haven't anything in that line, come back next week.' So off the man went, as he always did, down to a nearby harbour to watch the ships and feed the pigeons.

The following week the same thing happened, still no job, so off down to feed the pigeons. This carried on for three whole months, until one day the clerk informed him: 'I've got a job interview for you.' 'Where?' 'On some holiday island.' 'Isn't that a long way to go for a job?' 'Don't worry, you can't lose, it's all expenses paid so even if you don't get the job, it'll be a lovely day out.' 'I guess so,' said the man.

The next day, he set sail for this holiday island, but suddenly there was a freak storm and the ship sank, leaving him, the sole survivor, struggling in the water. Just then, a flock of pigeons were flying over in formation and he was spotted by the lead pigeon, which cooed to the other pigeons: 'Isn't that the guy who feeds us every week?' 'Yes it is,' they all cooed back. So they swooped down and towed him all the way to the holiday island.

Clambering up the beach, wet through to the skin, he found his way to the theatre where he asked the receptionist: 'May I see the manager?' The manager appeared, demanding to know what this dishevelled character was doing in his theatre. 'I've come for the job for a ballet dancer,' he explained. The manager hit the roof. 'Do you mean to tell me that you have the nerve to turn up for an interview with seaweed in your hair and a fish hanging out of your pocket!' 'I can explain,' the man said, 'Halfway across from the mainland, the ship sank and everyone except me drowned. Luckily for me, these pigeons came along and towed me all the way here.' 'In that case,' said the manager, 'I can't possibly give you the job.' 'Why's that?' 'Because we're definitely not looking for a pigeon-toed Ballet Dancer!'

FANCY THAT!

LATE ONE NIGHT two guys were drinking in a pub when it got to closing time. As they left, one of the guys, who had a hump on his back said: 'I'm going to take short cut home through the cemetery, are you coming with me?' 'No way!' replied the other guy turning to go home, 'I'll see you tomorrow night.'

The first guy was stumbling through the dark and eerie cemetery when suddenly the Devil leapt out in front of him. 'I'm the Devil!' he exclaimed, 'What have you got for me?' 'I haven't got anything,' the startled man blurted out, 'except my hump.' 'Right,' said the Devil, 'I'll have that!' There was a flash of lightning and the man's hump disappeared.

The next night, he walked upright into the pub and his mate hardly recognised him. 'What happened to you?' he asked. The man explained what had happened the night before, how the Devil himself had taken his hump away. 'You know, I've got a bad leg,' said his mate, 'Do you think it might work for me?' When the closing time bell went the two men got up to leave. 'This time I'll take the short cut,' said the mate. Soon afterwards he was staggering through the cemetery when, as he expected, the Devil leapt out in front of him. 'I'm the Devil! What have you got for me?' he demanded. 'Nothing,' came the reply, 'Only a bad leg.' 'Well,' said the Devil, sticking the other guy's hump on his mate's back, 'now you've got a hump as well.'

☺ ● ☺ ● ☺

THIS GUY PHONED the Guinness Book of Records. 'I wish to enter a record in your book,' he said, 'I've just completed a jigsaw puzzle in seven days.' The person on the other end of the phone asked: 'How do you know that's a record?' 'It has to be,' the guy replied, 'because on the box it states quite clearly: "8 to 10 years."'

DID YOU HEAR about the dyslexic, agnostic, insomniac who lay awake all night, wondering if there really was a dog?

☺ ● ☺ ● ☺

ONE DAY A man looked out into his garden and saw a strange looking woman, all dressed in white, waving a wand. 'I'm your fairy godmother,' she told him. 'I will grant you three wishes. What are they?' 'My first wish is to own a big mansion.' 'O.K. You shall have a big mansion.' 'My second wish is to own a Rolls Royce.' 'You shall have a Rolls Royce,' said the fairy. 'My third wish to win the National Lottery.' 'Your three wishes shall be granted, but only on one condition – if you spend the night with me.' The man didn't wish to jeopardise his dream come true so he spent the night with the fairy. Next morning, the fairy asked him: 'How old are you?' 'Thirty-three,' he replied. 'My goodness,' she said, 'thirty-three and you still believe in fairies!'

☺ ● ☺ ● ☺

ONE DAY, QUASIMODO asked for an apprentice to teach how to ring the bells at Notre Dame. The priest eventually found a boy suitable for the job and sent him up the stairs to the bell tower. 'Its quite easy,' Quasimodo explained, ' you just run at the bell and hit it with your head.' The boy did so, but the bell hardly rang. Quasimodo said: 'You'll have to run at it harder and faster.' The boy did, so much so that he bounced off the bell and over the tower wall, ending up flat on his face on the ground below. A big crowd had gathered around the boy, wondering who he was, when Quasimodo appeared. 'Do you know who this boy is?' asked one of them. 'Well,' Quasimodo replied, 'his face rings a bell!'

☺ ● ☺ ● ☺

PARTING SHOTS

A GUY WAS walking his dog along the banks of the River Thames when he caught sight of a man's head surfacing from the water and looking around in different directions When it caught sight of the man, the head called out, 'Could you direct me to the Tower of London?' 'Yes,' the guy replied, 'Just keep going down river until you reach Tower Bridge. It's quite a distance though.' 'Oh, that's alright,' shouted the head, 'I'm on my bike!'

☺ • ☺ • ☺

TWO INMATES WERE escaping from a mental hospital through a deep forest when they arrived at a very high brick wall. One inmate said to the other: 'You climb onto my shoulders and have a look over the wall to see what's over there.' After a very long wait he asked: 'Well, what can you see?' 'As far as I can see, its a nudist colony,' came the reply. 'A nudist colony!' he exclaimed, 'Well, is it men or women?' 'I don't know. None of them have got any clothes on!'

A MAN WAS walking around a museum when he suddenly came across a very large dinosaur. He stood looking at it with very deep interest when one of the attendants came up to him and enquired: 'Can I help you with any information on dinosaurs?' 'Oh, thank you,' said the man, 'can you tell me how old this dinosaur is?' 'Yes, it's one million years and ten months old.' 'How can you be so precise?' the man asked. 'Well,' replied the attendant, 'When I got this job, they told me this dinosaur was one million years old, and I've been here for ten months!'

☺ ● ☺ ● ☺

TWO ESKIMOS LIVING near the North Pole decided to go fishing. They both broke holes in the ice and cast their lines but, after some time had passed, one Eskimo hadn't caught a thing whilst his friend had loads of fish. 'How did you catch all those fish?' he called over. His friend mumbled something while keeping his mouth shut. 'I can't hear you. What did you say?' the Eskimo called. His friend mumbled something again with his mouth tight shut. 'I still can't hear what you're saying!' the Eskimo shouted. So his friend opened his mouth and hundreds of live maggots dropped out. 'I have to keep my mouth shut to so that all the maggots keep warm. That's how I've caught so many fish!'

☺ ● ☺ ● ☺

THE COMMITTEE OF a mental hospital were being shown around the building by a chargehand inmate. As they passed from room to room, he was explaining all the different activities, such as rugmaking, woodwork and pottery, which the other inmates were busily doing. One of the committee asked him: 'Can you do all these jobs?' 'Yes.' replied the chargehand. The visitor was very impressed and told him: 'You shouldn't be in here now. You should be released!' As they entered the last room, another committee member noticed an inmate hanging from the chandelier. He asked the chargehand: 'What's that man doing up there?' 'Oh,' he replied, 'That's a very sad story, he thinks he's an electric light bulb.' 'Can't you take him down?' the visitor asked. 'What,' the chargehand replied, 'and work in the dark!'

PARTING SHOTS 47

A GUY GOES into a railway station and walks up to the ticket office. 'A ticket to Jeopardy, please,' he asks. 'Jeopardy?' replies the booking clerk. 'Yes,' repeats the man, 'Jeopardy.' 'I'm sorry, sir,' says the booking clerk, thumbing through his big book, 'we haven't any such station or place listed.' 'You must have,' says the guy. 'I read in the newspaper only this morning that 300 jobs are in jeopardy.'

☺ • ☺ • ☺

OUT IN THE desert, the Red Indians captured the Lone Ranger. The Indian Chief told him: 'We're going to make you suffer,' and ordered his tribesmen to dig a deep hole in the desert sand and bury the Lone Ranger up to his neck. 'Now the sun will burn you up!' said the Chief. The Lone Ranger looked up and asked: 'Can I have a last request?' The Chief nodded and, with that, the Lone Ranger whistled loudly and out of the distance came galloping his horse, Silver. The horse lowered its head to the ground as the Lone Ranger whispered something in its ear. Immediately, the horse galloped off into the horizon, returning half an hour later with a cat in its mouth, which it dropped next to the Lone Ranger's head before turning and galloping off out of sight. The Lone Ranger looked up at the Chief. 'Can I have another last request?' he asked. 'You've already had one last request,' the Chief replied, 'but you may have just one more.' The Lone Ranger whistled and shouted: 'Hi, Ho, Silver.' A cloud of dust again appeared in the desert and Silver came galloping up to the Lone Ranger, lowering his head once more to listen to the Lone Ranger. The Lone Ranger turned and shouted angrily down Silver's ear: 'I told you to bring me a posse not a pussy!'

☺ • ☺ • ☺

A GUY GOES into his local shop where he'd bought a winning lottery ticket. 'I've come to claim my winnings,' he said to the shopkeeper. 'I'm awfully sorry,' the shopkeeper replied, 'but our computer's just gone down.' 'Right,' said the winner angrily, 'In that case I want my ticket money back!'

A COWBOY WAS riding his horse out on the prairie when he came across an old Indian, rocking back and forth on his chair, smoking a pipe of peace. 'Howdy Pardner!' he called over, ' I wonder if you could help me? I'm looking for some young squaws to have a good time with.' 'If you follow this trail for three miles,' the Indian called back, 'you'll come to the Indian reservation. Keep going until you reach IR3.' 'What's IR3?' 'It's the third wigwam and that's where all the best young squaws are.' 'Thank you pardner,' said the cowboy as he set off down the trail. Three days later, he returned. 'Thank you pardner,' he told the Indian, 'you were right. They were lovely squaws in IR3 and I had a wonderful time.' The Indian noticed the cowboy had bumps, bruises and cuts on his face and asked: 'What happened to you?' 'Well, I was having a great time when all of a sudden the FBI burst into the wigwam, battered me, and threw me out.' 'The FBI! The Federal Bureau of Investigation?' 'No,' said the cowboy, 'A Flipping Big Indian!'

☺ ● ☺ ● ☺

AN EXPLORER OUT in the depths of the African jungle came across a huge dead elephant and was busily looking over it when an African pigmy appeared on the scene. The explorer asked the pigmy: 'This elephant is one of the biggest I've ever seen, who killed it?' 'I did!' the pigmy replied. 'You did?' the explorer exclaimed, 'How?' 'With my staff.' 'With your staff? How big is it?' 'In all, 235, sir!'

☺ ● ☺ ● ☺

A FAMOUS INVENTOR was giving a lecture to a crowded school hall. When he had finished, he asked if there were any questions. One boy stood up and asked him: 'What, would you say, was the greatest invention of all mankind?' After a minute's pause, the inventor replied: 'In my opinion, the greatest invention of all mankind has to be Venetian Blinds.' The boy was puzzled, so he stood up again and asked: 'Why Venetian Blinds?' 'Well,' said the professor, 'without them, it would be curtains for all of us!'

101 SAYINGS

RIDDLES

What do you call a spider without any legs? A currant.

What's brown and sticky? A stick.

What's big and baggy? A bag.

What did the little strawberry say to the big strawberry?
'If we hadn't been in that bed together, we wouldn't be in this jam.'

RHYMES

Old Mother Hubbard, she went to the cupboard
to get her poor daughter a dress.
When she got there, the cupboard was bare
and so was her daughter, I guess.

I went to call on my best girl,
the bulldog jumped on me,
it bit me up the old back porch,
right up the maple tree.

Old Mother Hubbard, she went to the cave
to see her poor daughter Nancy.
When she got there, her daughter was bare,
just fancy!

Some girls put on corsets by scientific plan,
while others prefer to get their squeezing from a man.

Mary had a little watch,
she swallowed it one day.
Now she's taking Beechams Pills
to pass the time away.

Money cannot buy happiness after all is said and done,
but it surely can help to make the shopping much more fun.

Though I grew up with Fahrenheit,
on Celsius I would be sold,
if it applied to age
as well as hot and cold.

Don't worry if you work hard and your rewards are few,
remember the Mighty Oak was once a nut like you.

Bless this our house each brick and rafter.
May there always be good health and laughter.

Round Tuit, many times you've said,
I'll do it as soon as I get round to it.
Now is your chance, now you can do it
Now at last you've got a Round Tuit.

Women's faults are many, men have but two.
Everything they say and everything they do.

Thank God for dirty dishes, they have a tale to tell,
while others may go hungry we are eating very well.
With home, health and happiness, I should not want to fuss,
by this stark evidence, God's been very good to us.

Count your life by smiles, not tears.
Count your age by friends, not years.

Make new friends, but keep the old.
The new are silver, the old are gold.

As you go through life, two rules will never bend.
Never whittle towards yourself, nor pee against the wind.

Friend, there isn't a nicer wish to send
and I have found it true,
there isn't a nicer word than friend,
nor a nicer friend than you.

Wherever you wander,
wherever you roam,
be happy and healthy,
and glad to come home.

SOUND ADVICE

The only job which allows you to begin at the top is digging a hole.

The best and safest way to cut down on traffic accidents is to drive as if you owned the other car.

Sharp words create no friends; a few spoons of honey will always catch more flies than a whole gallon of vinegar.

Good humour and good health are most surely related, as one doctor declared: 'He who laughs last, lasts longer.'

You won't lose weight by talking about it. You have to keep your mouth shut.

The secret of contentment is to know how to enjoy what you have, while losing all desire for what is beyond your reach.

Your promise is the one thing you must keep after giving it to another.

Rumours are like cheques, don't endorse them until you're sure they're valid.

Advice given to others is like snow; the softer it falls, the deeper it sinks.

If you see someone without a smile, give him one of yours.

Plan ahead; it wasn't raining when Noah built the Ark.

Don't regret growing old, its a privilege denied to many.

Be happy, for every minute you are angry you lose 60 seconds of happiness.

'Yes' and 'No' are very short words, but we should think long before saying them.

Know the true value of time – snatch, seize and enjoy every minute.

FUNNIES

Of course my motor mechanic is good, if he wasn't why would I be going back to him every week?

To the very wise person who invented zero, thank you, kind sir, for nothing!

Did you hear about the fellow who called his car 'Flattery' because it got him nowhere.

Perhaps radar is spelt the same forwards and backwards so that policemen can catch speeding drivers both coming and going.

Eye-catching sign displayed in bicycle store window: WE NEED YOUR HELP IN PEDDLING THESE.

School days are the happiest of your life. Providing, of course, your children are old enough to go.

Get even. Live long enough to be a problem to your kids.

You would be happy too, if you could eat what bugs you.

101 SAYINGS   53

Blessed are they who go around in circles. For they shall be called the Big Wheels.

Dolphins are so intelligent that, within only a few weeks of captivity, they can train humans to stand at the very edge of the pool and throw them fish.

LIFE'S LIKE THAT

A budget is an orderly system of living far beyond your means.

You're an old-timer if you can remember when anyone who started a letter with 'Ms' either had a faulty typewriter or couldn't spell.

Perhaps the saddest event in a golfer's life is making 'a hole in one' without any witnesses.

One good way to learn about your neighbours is to entertain their children.

Too many of us spend too much time dreaming of the future, never noticing that a little bit of it arrives and then departs every day of our lives.

If we could locate other things as easily as we find fault, we would all get rich.

Liberty can never be absolute; it must be limited in order that everyone may share it.

It is very unlikely that anyone who gets stuck in a groove will ever make a record.

Our language is indeed strange – 'slow down' and 'slow up' mean the same thing.

The simplest toy any young child can operate is called a grandparent.

You can judge the character of a man by how he treats those who can do nothing for him.

If laughter is the best medicine, a grin must be second-best.

You're an old-timer if you can recall when patches on clothes meant poverty.

The main trouble with opportunity is that it only knocks, while temptation kicks the door in.

It would be easier to lose weight if replacement parts weren't so handy in the refrigerator.

A lot of trouble in this world is caused by combining a narrow mind with a wide mouth.

An umbrella is the only thing most people put away for a rainy day.

Middle age is when your mind starts making promises that your body can't always keep.

Nowadays you have to work like a dog to be able to live like one.

Why is there never enough time to do it right, but always enough time to do it over?

Character is what we are. Reputation is what people think we are.

The hurrier I go. The behinder I get.

There is no fool like an old fool; you just cannot beat experience.

It is nice to be important, but it is more important to be nice.

A bachelor is a rolling stone who gathers no boss.

When I do something right, no one remembers. When I do something wrong, no one forgets.

Kindness is a language which the deaf can hear and the blind read.

MARRIAGE LINES

Marriage is a great institution. For those who like institutions.

Marriage. It begins when you sink in his arms and ends with your arms in the sink.

A successful marriage requires falling in love many times over with the same person.

I am the boss in this house and I have my wife's permission to say so.

The opinions expressed by the husband in this house are not necessarily those of the management.

Many a woman has started out playing with fire and ended up cooking over it.

A woman who is smart enough to ask a man for advice is seldom dumb enough to take it.

To love and be loved is the greatest joy on earth.

Grow old along with me, the best is yet to be.

If a man has enough horse sense to treat his wife like a thoroughbred she will never grow into an old nag.

HOME SWEET HOME

Home is the place where we grumble the most and are treated the best.

No matter where I serve my guests, it seems they like my kitchen best.
A house is made of brick and stone, but a home is made of love alone.

Happy hearts make happy homes.

My house is clean enough to be healthy and dirty enough to be happy.

Breakfast, Lunch, Dinner or Tea,
Served in the kitchen seems more friendly to Me.

Kitchen closed on account of illness. I'm sick of cooking.

Home is where you can scratch wherever it itches.

Come in, sit down, relax, converse, our house doesn't always look like this, sometimes it's even worse.

All our visitors bring happiness. Some by coming, others by going.

A crust that is shared is finer food than a banquet served in solitude.

To know how sweet your home may be, just go away but keep the key.

PRAYERS

Bless this mess.

In my kitchen, bright and cheery, daily chores I will never shirk.
So bless this little kitchen, Lord, and bless me as I work.

Let me live in a house by the side of the road and be a friend to man.

A Mother's Prayer: 'Grant me patience. Oh Lord, but hurry!'

Lord, fill my mouth with worthwhile stuff and nudge me when I've said enough.

Oh Lord, help my words to be gracious and tender today, for tomorrow I may have to eat them.